CAPTAIN CONCUSSION

Quotes and Logic of an Interdimensional Pirate

by

Madison Christian Atteberry

DORRANCE
PUBLISHING CO
EST. 1920
PITTSBURGH, PENNSYLVANIA 15238

Dorrance Publishing Co
585 Alpha Drive
Suite 103
Pittsburgh, PA 15238
Visit our website at *www.dorrancebookstore.com*

ISBN: 979-8-88925-174-3
eISBN: 979-8-88925-674-8

I would like to thank all of you who have helped me
and Sarah Graves for the flag.

CAPTAIN CONCUSSION

Quotes and Logic of an Interdimensional Pirate

CAPTAIN CONCUSSION SAYS:

"James Solomon.

It's Captain 'James Solomon' Concussion…

I forgot to mention that on the title page…

Do-Do-Do…

Yay, fourth wall breaking is fun…

You… you can go on to the next page now.

I mean, you did buy this book,

so you might as well, you know, read it.

Go on now… go."

CAPTAIN CONCUSSION SAYS:

"To my banner, the 'phantom flag;

for any ship that has be taken or otherwise,

has it flown from its mast, shall lose its name

and become known as the Bloodlust!

…..

Wow, that was sort of badass."

CAPTAIN CONCUSSION SAYS:

"Good people. Never fear!

Your worst nightmare is here!"

CAPTAIN CONCUSSION SAYS:

"I wish to make a point against pacifism:

The point is my sword,

I'll be taking your stuff and you're not armed,

Get my point?"

CAPTAIN CONCUSSION SAYS:

"*sigh* I try so hard to make my day
a 'murder-free' day;
But there's always that one person
who has to ruin it."

CAPTAIN CONCUSSION SAYS:

"Roses are red,

Violets are blue,

You spilled my and my crew's beer,

And now we're going to guy you!"

CAPTAIN CONCUSSION SAYS:

"Common sense:

The only luxury that isn't taxed,

that literally everyone can buy,

And yet very few

CAPTAIN CONCUSSION SAYS:

"Hey… wait a minute!

This place has everything:

Legal and illegal drinking,

Legal and illegal drugs,

Legal and illegal gambling,

Legal and illegal prostitution,

And, AND loose women!

Whoa, all of the sudden…

I like going to church."

CAPTAIN CONCUSSION SAYS:

"If you have an idea that could make you money, act on it.

Never let any idea go to waste.

If you have an idea that can be sold whole or cut up

and sold separately to increase your wealth,

act on it.

You know… the drug dealer's method of making money."

CAPTAIN CONCUSSION SAYS:

"You know what….

Stealing a car from the gas station is a terrible idea.

I mean, the car is there to get refueled.

So what if you get in one with little or no gas?

Yeah…

I wish I had thought about that before jumping in this car."

CAPTAIN CONCUSSION SAYS:

"I like being self-employed,

because it's basically just a fancy way

of telling people that I'm unemployed."

CAPTAIN CONCUSSION SAYS:

"Some people think I don't have any fun in life;

Just work, work, work, and that's simply not true,

I just tell them,

Hey…

I have fun.

Why, I was once talked into a

three-way with a mermaid and a fairy;

SO FUCK YOU!"

CAPTAIN CONCUSSION SAYS:

"I believe in equality for all
and try to treat everyone the same…
LIKE THE FILTH UNDER MY BOOT!
Yeah, 'fair treatment' can go either way."

CAPTAIN CONCUSSION SAYS:

"For any crew that has a complaint,

please direct it to the predator-filled oceans

surrounding us that I have fondly come to call

THE COMPLANT DEPARTMENT!"

CAPTAIN CONCUSSION SAYS:

"To my loyal crew;

Many of you have been calling for a workers' union… aboard a 'pirate' ship…

Yom may have also noticed

that these people are no longer amongst us…

And by 'amongst us,' I mean, of course,

'amongst the living'.

I'm neither for nor against 'right to work,'

but I am for 'back to work';

So unless you want to meet their fate,

then I suggest you get BACK TO WORK!"

CAPTAIN CONCUSSION SAYS:

"There is no 'I' in team…

However, there is an 'M' and an 'E' which spells 'ME'!

And at the end of the day,

that is what this ship is all about.

So unless you want to find yourselves keelhauled,

then I suggest that you don't screw up your jobs!

Make-

Me-

MONEY!"

CAPTAIN CONCUSSION SAYS:

"Some people are herbivores,

others are carnivores, and me?

If I'm in the desert, I'm going to find meat;

If I'm in the jungle, I'm going to find meat <u>and</u> a salad!

Yeah, fuck your 'healthy living' and 'diet plans'

and all that 'real man' food!

ALL HAIL THE MIGHTY OMNIVORE!

WE SURVIVE BITCH!"

CAPTAIN CONCUSSION SAYS:

"Nations Unite against the United Nations!"

CAPTAIN CONCUSSION SAYS:

"The donkey is a smelly creature that is

known to be stubborn, carry lots of baggage,

noisy, by nature technically not supposed to exist,

and due to modern technology of transportation

and carrier drones, are largely obsolete…

yeah, that's pretty much sums up the Democrat party."

CAPTAIN CONCUSSION SAYS:

"The elephant is a large, smelly creature

that is known for its short temper,

going on a rampage resulting

in the wreckage of people's stuff,

formally a pack animal,

but due to modern technology of transportation

and carrier drones, are now largely obsolete,

oh, and on the verge of extinction.

Yep, that pretty much sums up the Republican party."

CAPTAIN CONCUSSION SAYS:

"How come all the people who should be in power

don't have the means to be in power,

and all the people who shouldn't be in power

have the means to be in power?

Something isn't quite right here."

CAPTAIN CONCUSSION SAYS:

"I'm a thief, pirate, smuggler, liar,

and all around bad person, but very honest about it… which sort of conflicts with the lying part

and I take responsibility for that…

which makes me more qualified to lead

then anyone in politics;

however, under my leadership and with me

being a criminal, things would most likely… improve?

…

VOTE CONCUSSION!"

CAPTAIN CONCUSSION SAYS:

"OH SHIT!

You're actually paying attention to me

and all the stupid shit I say?

WHY!?

Don't do that, I'm irresponsible!

That should have been evident from the <u>beginning</u>!"